LEGACY

FILL IN THE BLANK LIFE JOURNAL

About the writer:

I AM A CREATIVE FREE SPIRIT, WHO
ENJOYS LIFE TO THE FULLEST. I AM A
WIFE, GRANDMA, & MOM TO FOUR
BEAUTIFUL BLESSINGS. I AM THE
DAUGHTER OF TWO WONDERFUL
LOVING PARENTS. MY SIBLINGS INCLUDE
AN OLDER BROTHER, TWIN SISTER AND
YOUNGER SISTER.
MAKING MEMORIES MEAN SO MUCH TO
ME AND I WANTED TO PRESERVE THEM
FOR MANY YEARS TO COME. I HOPE YOU
ARE ABLE TO USE THIS AS A WAY TO
CAPTURE MEMORIES FOR YOU AND YOUR
FAMILY AS WELL.

Sharon Royice Smith

I was born on

_____

_____ in _____

_____

to _____

_____

I grew up in the town of _____

_____

My household consisted of, _____

_____

_____

_____

As a child I enjoyed things like...

_____

_____

_____

_____

I attended Elementary School at _____

_____ in _____

_____

I attended High School at _____

_____

in _____

_____

I attended College / Trade School at

_____

_____

in _____

Some of my proudest moments in life were....

_____

_____

_____

_____

_____

_____

_____

_____

Some fun facts:

I met your mom / dad at

_____

_____

I was __ when I learned to drive.

My first car was a

_____

My favorite color is

_____

_____

Growing up I had a pet ———————

named ————————————————————

My first job was ————————————

————————————————————————

————————————————————————

————————————————————————

My biggest pet peeve is

————————————————————————

————————————————————————

————————————————————————

PLACE PHOTO HERE

PLACE PHOTO HERE

My talents are

_____

_____

_____

My favorite holidays are

_____

_____

_____

_____

My favorite meal is

_____

_____

_____

_____

My first big purchase was

_____

_____

_____

_____

My strengths are

_____

_____

_____

_____

My fears are

_____

_____

_____

_____

I am passionate about

_____

_____

_____

_____

_____

_____

_____

_____

_____

_____

Ways that I give back to make the world a better place....

_____

_____

_____

_____

_____

_____

_____

_____

_____

_____

If I could fulfill my lifelong dream it would be....

_____

_____

_____

_____

_____

_____

_____

_____

_____

PLACE PHOTO HERE

PLACE PHOTO HERE

I'd say my happy place is...

_____

_____

_____

_____

I've always wanted to...

_____

_____

_____

_____

What were the Best / Worst of times?

You gave my life so much meaning because....

_____

_____

_____

_____

_____

_____

_____

_____

_____

_____

I'm proud of you because....

_____

_____

_____

_____

_____

_____

_____

_____

_____

I'm sorry if...

_____

_____

_____

_____

_____

Some of my favorite memories with you were....

_____

_____

_____

_____

I'd like you to know....

_____

_____

_____

_____

_____

_____

_____

_____

_____

_____

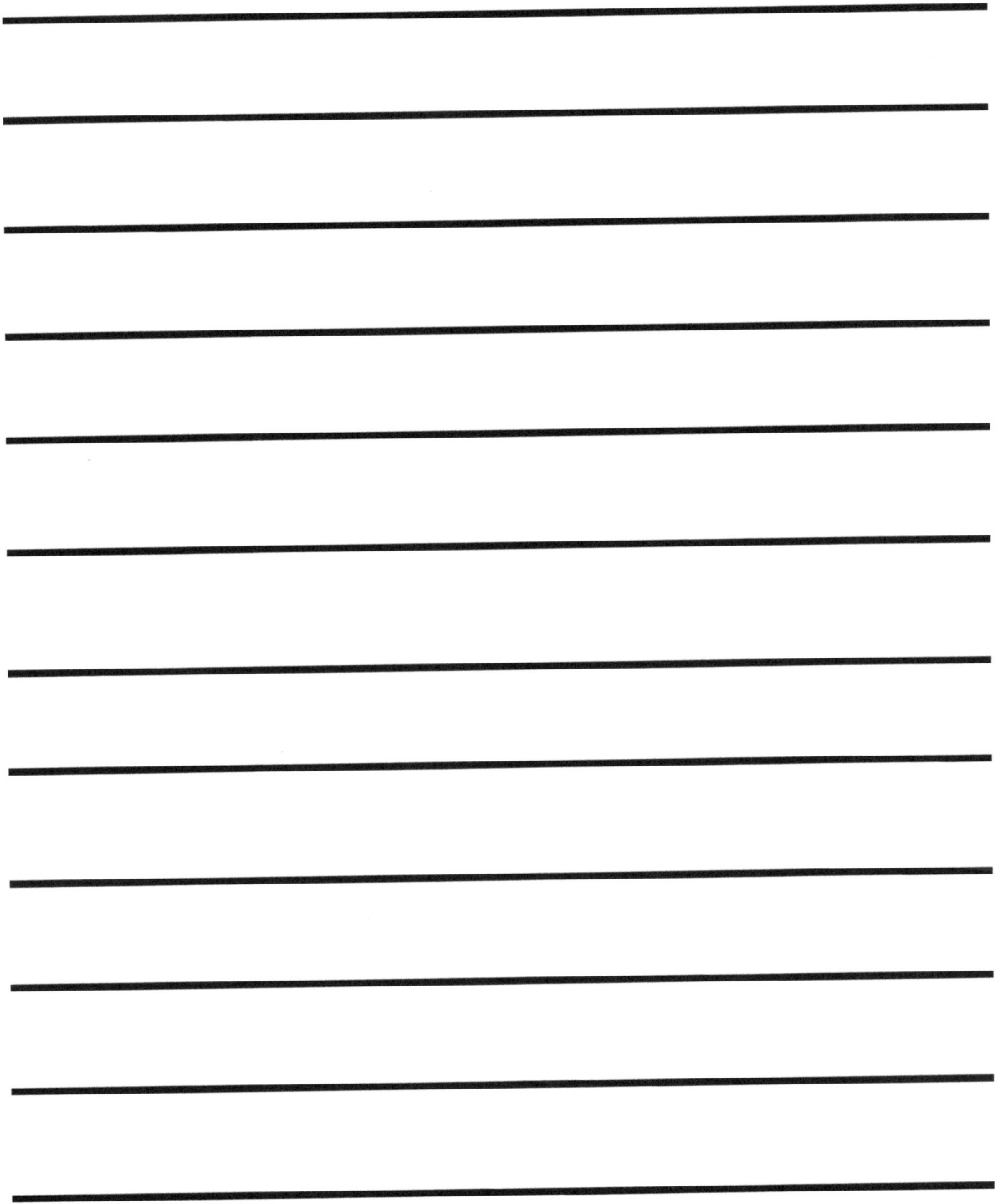

My wish for you would be...

_____

_____

_____

_____

_____

_____

_____

_____

_____

I'd like to be remembered by...

_____

_____

_____

_____

_____

_____

_____

_____

_____

_____

_____

Family Tree

HOW IT ALL BEGAN

I offer this little piece of me, so alone you'll never be... Although distance, time & space between, May the memories I leave be comforting...

With Love ♥

Written by:
Sharon Royice Smith

www.ingramcontent.com/pod-product-compliance
Lightning Source LLC
Chambersburg PA
CBHW040256100426
42811CB00011B/1287